Rim to Rim
Ada Shaw

Thanks to my editor, Rick Barry for making this a reality, to my mother, Jennifer Shaw for pushing me to write this in the first place, and to my Uncle Tim, for taking a 13-year old through the Grand Canyon.

Table of Contents

1. Forward
2. Notes from the Trail-- Pre-hike
3. My Backpacking Story
4. Why I Am in the Grand Canyon in the First Place
5. Finally, The Big Day Arrives
6. Notes from the Trail-- Roaring Springs
7. Day 2--Phantom Ranch
8. Day 3-- Indian Gardens
9. Notes from the Trail--Leisure Time at Indian Gardens
10. Day 4-- The South Rim
11. The Finish
12. Final Observations

Forward

I wrote this book several years ago when I was thirteen years old. The idea came to me when I was in the Hermit's Rest gift shop in Grand Canyon National Park reading books by authors who write in several different styles. My mom came across a short chapter book.

She turned to me and said, "Ada, you can write a book like that."

Of course, since she is my mother, I immediately rolled my eyes at her and said, "No thanks."

I was thirteen and defiant. But eventually, the promise of fame and fortune arose in my mind and I thought, "Okay, why not? What can I possibly lose by simply writing?"

So, I packed a little journal in my backpack as we headed down into the canyon and wrote my little heart out at the end of each day. Of all the moments spent down in the canyon, some of the best were the quiet ones, sitting on the porch of the ranger station where we were staying, writing, listening to nature's sounds, and absorbing every bit of the canyon's essence I could.

Those four days were inspiring, as they should have been, and I found myself trying to capture it on paper. I've always been a decent writer, but the task of recalling every magical moment on the trail was daunting, and at the end of a hot day, it's not necessarily the first thing I felt like doing. I was pretty faithful, though, and I wrote down everything I could remember from the moment I woke up to the moment I sat down to write.

Each day I split my writing task into two sections. The first part would be about all the things that had happened already: the people I'd met, the events of the day, any unfortunate circumstances that arose. This was important to me because I was well aware of how details slip your mind just hours after an event, and I wanted to remember everything. I worked hard to recall each day as accurately as I could, so I would be able to preserve them forever on paper. Then, when that hard work was over, I would relax and try to capture the very moment in time I was sitting there, describing the sights, the sounds, the smells and the emotions running through my head. This was my favorite time as I could tune into nature, observe, and really be in the moment.

Later, in my editing, these split sections became a dilemma for me. I now had a book, but it was in two different tenses. Somehow, I had to figure out how to fix that. Assuming that you're going to read the book, you will soon learn that I didn't fix it. That is because I think the pieces written in the present tense were richer staying where they were -- in the moment. The parts that are in the present tense are what I call "Notes from the Trail." Truly, they are not notes from the trail, but notes from off the trail, which were just as much a part of my journey as was the trail itself.

My rim-to-rim hike lasted only a long weekend, but the memories lasted much longer than just those four under-planned days of walking, thinking, listening, and observing. During this time, I became more acutely aware of the joys of trail friends, hard work, and pushing through discomfort or pain for a sense of accomplishment. Let me tell you, there is nothing like lying down listening to the chirping cicadas after walking six hours in the hot sun. Everything feels better after completing such hard work. Food? Better. Water? Better. Sleep? Much better. I learned about living simply and being happy with that.

And now I'm glad I'll get to share these experiences with you. Please, consider hiking the Grand Canyon. It's a breathtakingly beautiful place. It's a lot of work, but, trust me, it's worth it. Whatever "wow factor" you get from looking over the rim, it pales in comparison to what you will feel when you have walked down those walls and seen the canyon from the inside-out.

Enjoy.
Ada Shaw
February 2016

Rim to Rim

May 2014
Notes from The Trail-- Pre-Hike

The scene of my adventure was forming long before I can even guess. It began taking shape more than five million years ago, before the dinosaurs and way before the cavemen appeared. All along, through evolution, new discoveries and civilization, it was forming. Sure, it was slow in forming, but slow and steady can create perfection. It took those millions of years for the Colorado River to carve that majestic furrow through the layered bedrock. This place began mysteriously and softly, and to this day it is a wondrous creation in progress.

My adventure: hiking the Grand Canyon.

I am thirteen years old and in two days, I'll be deep in the canyon, surrounded by nature, and probably sore down to my bones. I'll be in an adventure that thousands have conquered before me, yet few of the millions who visit each year have done. What I will do may seem ordinary in the grand scheme of things. (I couldn't help the pun.) But, it is extraordinary in my small world, and if you decide to participate in this adventure, it will be extraordinary for you, too. So, what is all this big talk about? The Grand Canyon Rim-to-Rim Hike!

Throughout the past ten days I've been at the Grand Canyon, I've studied the trail from the south rim in order to get an idea of where I'll be spending three nights. As I've been observing, I've noticed mule trains, day hikers in flip flops, toddlers hiking and runners sweating profusely. Along with everyone else and the daily crazies are the regular backpackers like me who just want to enjoy their time in the canyon and the hard work of backpacking through it.

My Backpacking Story

My pink backpack serving me well on the trip

My love for backpacking began soon after I could walk. My parents tell me that when I was just two or three I'd take a bag and drag it around the house, all day, every day. My parents didn't know why I did this, but they thought it was pretty comical. I had assembled so much stuff it was ridiculous. I was hauling three containers around, one of them being a laundry basket full of clothes, just in case, you know, there was an occasion for an impromptu costume change or something. Since then, I've learned how to trim down my pack a bit.

I grew up in Middleville, a small town in southwestern Michigan. Middleville is near an outdoor recreational area called Yankee Springs.

Throughout my early childhood (four to ten years old), my family would take hiking trips out there on weekends and vacations, as well as hike along Lake Michigan, which I always looked forward to. What I never knew was that there was an even better and bigger way to hike. It was called "backpacking." Then, one fateful day (or at least I thought so at the time), my parents announced we were moving. Basically, I thought my world was ending. But in fact, it was really just beginning -- because I found "Goodwillie."

Goodwillie Environmental School in Forest Hills Public Schools is an environmental school for fifth- and sixth-grade students. It is one of those really awesome schools you might hear about on a PBS station, but dismiss because you think the kids are just talking it up. But let me tell you, this is the real deal. Every year about 150 students apply, but only 50 are accepted. The process they go through to admit people is long and arduous. It's for kids who really love nature, who are happiest outdoors, and who are capable of working independently. From the first day my mom heard of this school in our new district, she said, "This school is for Ada."

She kept saying it and I kept believing it. Pretty soon, I had no doubt I was going to get in, even if the odds were slim. But, that didn't matter to me. I already knew that I was meant for this school, that *this school* was always meant to be a part of my life. It felt like my whole being was driven to this singular opportunity.

Memorial Day weekend rolled around and I had been hearing rumors that this was about the time that the letters arrived revealing our fate regarding Goodwillie. On the Thursday before the four day weekend, I got a call from my mom. That's right, *the* call; the letter had arrived. We rushed home from school to open it, and although I had little doubt that I would get in, I was a little nervous when the "what ifs" crept into my head. But, I need not have worried. The letter said, "Congratulations, you have been accepted into GES."

During my fifth and sixth grade years at Goodwillie, I started to fall in love with backpacking more and more. For spring break of sixth grade my family drove down to Georgia and hiked the approach trail to the Appalachian Trail, and stayed at Hike Inn, a lodge that you can only access on foot. During that trip, I got it in my head that I wanted to hike the *whole* "A.T." – all 2,167 miles -- not just fourteen miles of it.

After my Appalachian inspiration, I began to ask to go hiking after school and on weekends. We would drive out to Goodwillie, and hike trails through the 400-acre county park adjacent to it, Seidman Park. Sometimes I would join my mom and her friend Shana for their "extreme" hikes, and I thoroughly enjoyed those hours in nature.

Those two years at Goodwillie Environmental School were some of the best of my life. They flew by so fast, and pretty soon it was the end of sixth grade and time for the last big activity, the famous "Spring Camp." We'd heard rumors about it, and whenever alumni would come back to visit, they would always say their favorite memory was this last week of school. We had to take a huge test on survival skills, and get a 95 percent score or higher on it to be able to go.

The itinerary for this big trip was three days backpacking, three days canoeing, and we had to be prepared for everything from hypothermia to heat stroke. I passed the test and the teachers split us into two groups, half the people started out canoeing, the other half backpacking. I was lucky enough to be with almost all my friends, and backpacking on the first leg of that adventure. This was my first *true* backpacking experience, and what a great way to spend it: in the Nordhouse Dunes Wilderness Area, barefoot in the soft warm sand of Lake Michigan's beach. What could be better?

    We probably only hiked about three miles the first day, but it seemed a lot farther since the arches in my feet began to feel like they were collapsing. We set up camp behind a dune with the lake right over the hill. For three days, it was only hiking, eating backpacking food, drinking filtered water from Lake Michigan and camping and telling stories around the campfire. That was when I began to have dreams of doing this *way* more often.

The summer before seventh grade I was in a downer-mood because I had to go back to regular school the upcoming year, a big step down from Goodwillie. Luckily, we took a couple of awesome trips to northern Michigan and I forgot all my worries.

We never really backpacked that summer because we didn't have any supplies yet, and my parents weren't ready to make the transition from car camping to backpacking. But, we took a couple of killer hiking trips, including South Manitou Island (ten miles in one day) in Sleeping Bear Dunes National Lakeshore. South Manitou is an island in Lake Michigan. The only way to get there is by ferry, about an hour's trip from Leland. But when you do get there, 300-foot dunes tower over the huge lake's deep blue water, tall trees provide cool shade, and long beaches allow for world-class swimming experiences.

One day in December, when we were at Bill and Paul's, a local outdoor apparel shop, my mom suggested we look at backpacks, just for the heck of it. I took one look at the shelf stocked fully with every size and shape of pack and suddenly, I needed one. I was overcome with a terrible desire, and there was one that looked the perfect size for me: small, sturdy, and (although not my first color preference) pink. I decided I needed that backpack more than I needed anything else, and I set my mind on buying it. I'm impulsive, so I would have pulled money I didn't know I had out of my pocket to buy it, but my mom slowed me down saying she needed to "think about it." But, my passionate love for that particular backpack had already been sparked, and there was no stopping me.

One day later, that pack was all mine.

Why I Am in the Grand Canyon in the First Place

My Uncle and me on the North Kaibab Trail

One summer day before seventh grade, while my mom was driving me through the lush countryside of Michigan, she asked me, "How would you like to take a semester off during seventh grade and travel?" In all honesty, the idea terrified me. No friends, no basketball, no school. Trust me, it sounds like all fun and games until you seriously consider doing it, but when it gets real, it's a scary idea, and I wasn't ready for such a big change.

Eventually, my mom convinced me it would be great fun, so she planned a "semester abroad." My mom, sister and I took a semester and traveled to Costa Rica, Ireland, and of course, the Grand Canyon. My Dad had to stay behind due to his job, but we Skyped him every day and he was excited that we got to experience new cultures, experiences and ideas as a part of our education. My two older siblings, Ali and Anisa, were both in college and it wasn't possible for them to join us.

In Costa Rica, we stayed with my grandparents at their house near San Vito and were completely immersed into a different culture. We took this time to learn Spanish and about the people and ecosystems of that beautiful country. After 75 days we flew back to Michigan, and had three weeks to recover before flying to Phoenix, Arizona. While we were preparing for our trip out west, my uncle called and invited me, just me, on a rim-to-rim hike. His wife had completed this hike, but my Uncle Tim had never had the chance. Knowing that I loved to backpack, he saw this as a great opportunity for both of us. When my mom asked me if I was interested, I replied with an enthusiastic "Yes! Yes! Yes! Just say yes and ask him how much weight I have to carry and I will start training right away!"

I filled my pack with shoes so it weighed fifteen pounds. I thought that was a good weight to start with. My mom would take me to different hiking paths near our home and we would hike three to five miles in preparation for my trip.

Those three weeks in Michigan flew by and before we knew it, we were boarding another plane and heading west. Uncle Tim and his one-year-old daughter met us at Phoenix Sky Harbor International Airport. We immediately drove about six hours until we finally made it into Grand Canyon National Park, which is where he lived. He and his wife were law-enforcement rangers at the south rim of the Grand Canyon, so we planned on spending seventeen days getting to know them, our new cousin, Arizona, and the canyon better.

    The hike was on my mind all that time. We had arrived on May 6, but we were not starting our hike until May 16. Even though we had ten days together before our hike, only within the last two days did everything come together. We took a day-trip to Flagstaff, Arizona for our food and supplies, and sent them off Monday night on the "pack and fly," which is a mule train that carries supplies down into the canyon to the ranger stations there. The next day, Tuesday, we began our hike.

Finally, the Big Day Arrives

The "before" picture

At 5:30 a.m. my mom woke me up just enough for me to know that I wasn't sleeping any longer. About five minutes later I reluctantly went into the living room, careful not to wake my younger sister who was sharing a room with me. My Uncle Tim was already awake, but was still in his bathrobe. He had been up for a while trying to slim down our packs. We decided on eggs and cheese for a protein-rich breakfast, so my mom cooked them while we finished our last-minute preparations. By 6:25 we were loaded up into my Uncle Tim's SUV, and my mom was pulling out of the driveway, she had to drive my Uncle and me to the shuttle pickup. By 6:28 my Uncle and I were in the parking lot of the Bright Angel Lodge where we were to catch our shuttle to the North Rim. The van arrived at exactly 6:30, so my mom took a quick "before" picture, and sped off, back to my Uncle's house where my sister, Aunt and little cousin were still sound asleep. Uncle Tim and I hurried over to load our packs into the vehicle. It turns out that only three other people were along for the ride. Two of them were brothers, and the other one was their friend (who was also a man), so that made me the youngest person and the only girl.

    We moved out of the park pretty quickly, mainly because our chauffeur was a pretty terrible driver. In order to get to the North Rim of the Grand Canyon from the South Rim, it's about a 4 hour drive, even though it's all technically one park. The problem is, the only way to get across the Colorado river and to the other rim of the Grand Canyon, is to go across the Navajo Bridge that is on the Native American reservation. For about two hours we drove through the reservation that is adjacent to the park. Then, we crossed Navajo Bridge and soon after, entered the North Kaibab National Forest. There were towering cliffs above us, and our driver sped up on all the turns and curves as we made our way upward. I was thinking back to Costa Rica, and how crazy the drivers were there, when suddenly one of the brothers in front of me mentioned Costa Rica. I had a feeling we were both thinking about it because of the curvy roads, the bad driving, and the fear we would very likely drive off a cliff at any moment.

When he was finished telling his story, I told him that I had just come back from living there for seventy-five days. We talked about Manuel Antonio National Park, rice and beans, the roads, and a few other shared experiences. We pulled over at the Jacob Lake Motel and Gas Station for a quick stop and we were back speeding along the road before we knew it. Then, *boom*, we were in the national park at the North Kaibab trailhead. We thanked our driver and wished good luck to our fellow passengers, who were planning to accomplish the entire Rim-to-Rim Hike in one day (which you should only do if you're *insane*). They gave us the rest of their bagels, so we ate those and trail mix for lunch. We took turns in the bathroom one last time before Tim and I headed down.

Starting at the North Kaibab Trailhead, at an elevation of 8,250 feet, the hiking felt relatively easy, mostly because we were going downhill. I began to notice that my senses sharpened, and I was able to hear, smell and see everything more clearly than before. When I told my Uncle that everything seemed super well-defined, he said, "kind of like an Imax movie?" I laughed and agreed.

As we walked, we had a couple of people ask us how far it was to the top, but we mainly just exchanged smiles and nods with other hikers and continued walking, while watching our footing. There were a couple of times we decided to stop for a break. About three-quarters of a mile below the rim we stopped at Coconino Overlook, where we met a man using the overlook to watch for his brother who had left the South Rim at 4:00 a.m. that morning.

At one point, I had the privilege of going to the bathroom in an outhouse (as opposed to against a cliff) before hiking through the cool, windy, Supai tunnel.

    About two miles below the rim, we ran into a ranger named Della who was nice, talkative, and super happy to see us. She's a law enforcement ranger who helps people out and enforces rules on the trail (she and my uncle work together, so they knew each other). Many people were asking her questions so we had to leave her without much more conversation.

Just beyond Red Wall Bridge that crossed what looked like a dried-up creek bed, we took another break, took our shoes off, and ate a couple of Pringles. We got back up and continued hiking, not realizing we had five miles to go until we reached the ranger station that was our ending point for the day. At some points the cliffs were straight up and down on either side of the trail. No bathroom breaks there. Finally, we reached a sign that said:

<-Roaring Springs
Cottonwood->.

Since the ranger station is called Roaring Springs, we assumed we took the trail that led us to the left. After about half a mile with no signs of rangers, we turned around, passed the sign again, and went toward Cottonwood. We passed a small side trail that headed toward a building we thought was the ranger station. The path was a little sketchy but we figured, "Ah, what the heck, they probably just didn't want people to annoy them." After a few close calls on that almost non-existent trail we finally reached the … helipad and pump-house thing. And what did I do? I just laughed and laughed, because I just couldn't think of anything else to do. And because we had just gone off on a "sketch-ball trail" (as my uncle called it) for nothing. We just sat there on the empty helipad for probably fifteen minutes, our egos a little bit bruised, and our feet *a lot* bruised. I just lay there and laughed and Uncle Tim simply laid down on the hard concrete, content for the moment just to listen to the sounds of the desert. After about twenty minutes, we scrambled our way back along that small side trail and continued walking on the main trail towards Cottonwood/Roaring Springs (at this point we weren't sure if those were two different places or not). Not long after that, we happily saw the ranger station and unloaded on its front porch. We had hiked about 6.5 miles, and descended more than 4,000 feet on our first day.

The ranger who lived here, Betsy, was also super nice and very glad to have company. Most people have to reserve a spot at the campgrounds for the night, but since my Uncle is a ranger, we got the special privilege of sleeping at the ranger stations. However, I also noticed two other hikers had planted themselves on the helipad. They "made camp" there, and stayed through the night, sending out some real carefree camp vibes that I happily soaked in.

That night, after a hearty meal of macaroni and cheese and hotdogs, we slept on the floor of the front porch of the ranger station and looked at the stars, listened to the musical humming of insects, birds, the rush of the wind and water flowing down nearby creeks, all coming together. Right before falling out of consciousness I saw a scorpion crawl across my field of vision, but I was too tired to care and simply drifted off to sleep.

    The night was a little chilly and we didn't have sleeping bags, only sleeping mats under us and thin sheets to cover us, but around 1:00 a.m., I saw the full moon rise over the canyon, which made it all worth it. I woke up on and off all night long and at 3:00 a.m. I moved off the porch to look at the stars. Wow! They were amazing! I saw the big dipper, Hercules, and other constellations I thought I recognized. There were four shooting stars, and one went so far it went all the way behind a cliff! At 3:30 I just started to smile uncontrollably because I thought to myself, "How did I ever get so lucky to be sleeping outside, under the stars, in the middle of the Grand Canyon?"

Notes from the Trail -- Roaring Springs

Sitting on the front porch of the Roaring Springs Ranger Station, you could be looking at any creek in the world. That's because the cliff behind the creek is only about twenty-five feet tall, and the trees hide the rest of the canyon. There's a helipad between the porch and the creek flowing through Roaring Springs, the only thing connecting us to the outside world.

The porch is about forty feet long, and maybe nine feet wide. It is shared by two different residences. You can barely hear anything above the soothing sound of that nearby creek. Earlier, it was very silent and the insects made what sounds there were. The vibe here is really cool. Imagine a summer evening at a cottage. Now crank up the sound of the water, and imagine you hiked all day to get there. That's how it feels. It's quite relaxing after a full day of hiking.

Day 2 -- Phantom Ranch

Ribbon Falls

After watching the full moon rise, I finally fell asleep again at 3:30 a.m., and it seemed like two minutes until the alarm started ringing at 5:00. I woke up Uncle Tim, who had gone inside at four o'clock to get more comfortable, and we made a quick toasted breakfast, which included pop tarts, waffles, and English muffins. Betsy was up shortly after us and headed out before we got a chance to talk to her. We cleaned up, packed up, and by 6:20 we were on the trail. Immediately we saw Betsy and another ranger. We thanked Betsy for letting us stay the night, said goodbye, and continued walking. Quickly we came upon a fork in the trail, and we opted for the road less traveled -- a quarter-mile side trail to Ribbon Falls.

The falls were amazing! This waterfall was a hundred feet high and pouring onto a moss-covered, hollow, cone-shaped rock. We brought our packs up to the top of the waterfall and ate a snack there. Then we just hung around, getting wet to cool off and observing people and nature co-existing.

Water fell over a cliff, onto the top of the cone where it had worn a small pool. Then, the pool at the top would overflow and run down the moss-covered sides of the rock. You could stand underneath that cliff and watch it gather in the pool, then slide down into another pool farther below. It was ten degrees cooler in an area behind the waterfall, and beyond beautiful.

    After about an hour we put our packs on and walked back to the main trail. It turned out we took the long cut that goes up a huge, unnecessary hill. On the trail, a lady running in the opposite direction told us that there were rattlesnakes just up on the trail ahead, and we, in exchange, told her about the short-cut we didn't take.

    Then, we continued walking.

    For a second, we pulled off the trail to take a break and re-apply sunscreen. Then, we continued walking.

    There was an Asian couple, with limited English, we continually passed, playing a sort of flip-flop game with them for several hours. So, we became "trail friends." We stopped at the only shaded place for miles and they came in to join us.

They asked us in broken English, "Did you stay at Cottonwood last night?"

We replied, "yes, we did."

The lady said, "That's better."

Then they asked, "Are you staying at Phantom Ranch tonight?"

Once again, we replied, "Yes, we are."

The lady said, "That's better."

Finally they asked, "How many days are you taking?"

We replied, "Four."

The lady said, "That's better."

It turned out that they were doing it all in one day and the lady thought our plan was much better.

We walked through a creek-created "hallway" leading us through the towering canyon, with walls of rock going 1,000 feet straight up from the creek bed. While making our way through this corridor, we stopped, numb with exhaustion, overheated, and wincing at blistering feet, and lay, fully clothed, in Bright Angel Creek. I slipped off my beloved backpack and hiking boots and slid on my sandals before putting my feet against some rocks in the shallow creek. I lay down on my back and let the current run over my hair, face and clothes.

My Uncle Tim cooled himself off by dipping his camouflaged mesh cloth into the creek and wrapping it around his neck. A runner saw us cooling off and felt inspired to jump in, so he did, completely submerging his body, backpack, shoes and all and lay in the water for about five minutes. When he finally stood up, he yelled, "I have no shame!" and continued running along the trail. After we were done laughing at the absurdity of the past moment, we got up, squeezed our clothes to ring out the water, and put our hiking boots back on.

Then, we continued walking.

A while later, when all our adrenaline was failing us and spirits were low, a woman told us we were almost to Phantom Ranch without us even asking the question. Hope reawakened. So around each bend you could hear me telling Uncle Tim, "I bet it'll be around the next corner." And as each bend came, my hope failed to dwindle and I continued to exclaim, "Oh, it's definitely right around that next corner." Or, "I mean, it should be coming up soon; there's a good chance it's around that next bend." But each time it just wasn't there!

Finally, (and I do mean "finally," as in "after an hour or two of hardcore, home-run hiking") we came to a sign that said "Welcome to Phantom Ranch." Every muscle in my body was relieved that we had (finally) arrived. We passed the Asian couple one last time and found the ranger station with no trouble at all. Erika, a ranger there, was very welcoming and made us Tang slushies.

Then I ate four clementines and a Power Bar.

 I had imagined Phantom Ranch as a hotel, and on the south side of the Colorado River. But, it ended up having more of a summer camp feel and is on the north side of the river. An assortment of tents lined the crystal clear creek in designated campsites, and the cottonwoods growing along the water were strung with hammocks. There were a few cabins and dorms located at the site of Phantom Ranch, but we never saw them as we passed through. It was a super-hot 99.9 degrees, but luckily we were able to sit inside the air-conditioning of the ranger station as soon as we arrived. Immediately my trail-adrenaline faded, and I was in need of a nap and some stretching.

Eventually I fell into a deep sleep of pure exhaustion. It was about six o'clock when I finally zonked out, and at 8:30, my uncle woke me up for a stir-fried dinner with brown rice, peppers, and corn. While I ate, I listened to two rangers talk, who I hadn't seen earlier, and it seemed like one of them was also doing a rim-to-rim hike.

Right after dinner, I put together a sleeping pad and pillow, and lay out under the stars for about five minutes. The temperature was a perfect 70 degrees, and soon I fell asleep, sleeping the best I had in years.

Day 3 -- Indian Gardens

The bridge where we crossed Colorado River

I didn't wake up once in the middle of that night. At 4:00 the alarm clock went off. Then I got up, got ready, ate breakfast, and packed the proper food for the day in my pack. We sent back seventeen pounds of food from Phantom Ranch to the rim where we would pick it up at the end of our hike. The same mules that had brought the food down would take the extra back up (sorry, mules)!

On our way out, we passed someone sleeping on a picnic table who I recognized from the ranger station the previous night. Soon we crossed the Colorado River on a tall suspension bridge. For a while after that we hiked along the riverbank, and finally we turned in toward the South Rim and continued hiking along Bright Angel Creek on the Bright Angel Trail.

In my opinion, this part of the trail was the prettiest by far; on some sections I felt like I was climbing up a mountain, not out of a canyon. Humidity from the Colorado River struck me by surprise in the early morning, and I continued to exclaim over and over again that the atmosphere felt like Florida, a big change from the Phoenix-like air of yesterday. My uncle continued to remind me that we were in Arizona, but that didn't stop me from sharing my enthusiastic opinion every few minutes.

Bright Angel Creek had several small waterfalls flowing over beautiful smooth red rock. Millions of years had polished these rocks to an almost glass-like sheen that stunned me by their beauty. On one of those waterfalls, I was taking a cool-down and my favorite Goodwillie water bottle slipped out of my backpack and floated down a three-foot waterfall. Just as it was about to fall down another series of waterfalls that probably led straight to the Colorado river, I scooped it up and gave it a hug. That was a very close call, too close.

    After turning toward the canyon face, the climb wasn't too bad for the first couple of minutes until the trail shot abruptly straight up. After that, we never caught a break with a stretch of flat land.

Before ascending, we stopped at a cave to eat and take a break. As we were sitting there, enjoying our trail mix, a lady ran over, took a pee in plain sight, and continued running. I was a little mortified, but she never even noticed us.

We continued walking and the views got better and better, the trail winding its way up a wall that from any distance looked like it was straight up. I can't remember whether we stopped for a break, or if the world just slowed down, but I distinctly remember the very moment when I turned around and looked over at the incredible view, all of which we had just hiked, and in that moment, feeling my whole perspective change. To some, that moment might not be their highlight, but for me something happened: the atmosphere shifted, and I just saw the earth in all its simplicity and wonder.

As we continued, I'd stick my hair in the creek every once in a while to cool off. The water would run down my back and get my shirt wet for about thirty minutes before the sun would evaporate it completely off. The last mile or so was breathtaking, consisting of miniature cliff overhangs, which reminded us of Mesa Verde National Park... but hobbit-sized. The creek led us all the way to the Indian Gardens Ranger station.

We arrived just in time to see a helicopter land. Uncle Tim knew some of the people who were in charge and asked them what was going on. Helicopters don't always mean someone rich and famous is arriving, and in the Grand Canyon they often signal that a dire situation is at hand. Apparently, a lady hurt her leg so badly she had to be flown out. I was privileged to watch the ranger-paramedics put the injured lady in the helicopter and take off, waving goodbye as they swooped close overhead and headed up towards the rim.

There was one other person there with me, watching the helicopter leave, and I recognized her from the trail earlier. We introduced ourselves and I found out that she knows most of the rangers because she comes down here almost every weekend out of her love for the canyon.

I headed back into the ranger station and read for about half an hour then cuddled up (*literally* cuddled, although not intentionally) with the book, "Red Pyramid," as I fell asleep. I slept from about noon to three, then came out on the porch with Uncle Tim. We both wrote for a while. Eston, a ranger, talked to us for a bit. Two girls, both about eleven, were also hiking from rim-to-rim and were working on becoming Junior Rangers. Eston made us chocolate chip cookies which were warm and very yummy!

At about four in the afternoon, the sun was slanted at the perfect angle, and all the rock layers of the Grand

Canyon's walls stood in stark contrast with each other. It was about 81 degrees at the Indian Garden Ranger Station, but in the shade there was a nice breeze and a cool place to rest. It's funny, because I was wearing long pants and a light sweatshirt; most people, especially from Michigan, would consider it to be hot out at that temperature, but after hiking down near Phantom Ranch, it felt cool to me. I sat on the porch looking out over the trails, reveling in the cool breeze and thinking about the new perspective I'd gained from the inner canyon.

    That night Uncle Tim made fettuccini with alfredo sauce and green beans which we shared with a few hikers from Canada, two rangers, and one paramedic. We had a huge plate of cookies which were picked at throughout the night. We enjoyed each other's company. Uncle Tim and I each claimed a couch and slept until the crack of dawn.

Notes from the Trail -- Leisure Time at Indian Gardens

As I look across the Canyon towards Roaring Springs from this ranger station, I know what it actually looks like, and it looks nothing like it does from the rim. It's not colorless rock, but a desert with blooming wildflowers and cactus in abundance.

There are a variety of plants here because of the availability of water from the nearby stream counteracting the general dryness of the desert. There is a garden of cactus along the walk up to this porch, but there are also tall trees, mostly cottonwoods, that provide the pleasant shade. I spent about fifteen minutes trying to identify a tree to my left, and finally I found out that it was a velvet ash, which also has other names such as Arizona ash or desert ash. It's the most common ash species in Arizona. It grows to a height of thirty feet with a trunk that is one foot in diameter. That's pretty big for the desert. This tree is still young, but soon it will provide good protection from the sun.

Day 4- The South Rim

Relaxing at Indian Gardens

We woke up and were ready to go by 6:20. We hit the trail trying to beat the heat, even with our "late" start. As we climbed the Grand Canyon wall one step at a time, ascending 3,000 feet in three miles, I was feeling strong. This seemed easier than the downhill climb we started with. I had a strong desire for an ice cream cone at trail's end that kept me going.

About a mile below the South Rim, I was walking with my head down, watching my footing, when I looked up and saw a mob of people heading down the trail toward us. I thought I recognized two of them, but dismissed the thought for a moment. Then I realized it really was my mom and my sister coming down to escort us up to the top of the South Rim. I smiled, surprised, and quickened my pace to go greet them.

My mom had been watching for days too many people completing their hikes in dire condition, collapsing and needing medical attention at the top of the south rim. Her fears had escalated as an increasing number of people barely made it to the top before succumbing to heat stroke and sheer exhaustion. She couldn't believe how strong my uncle and I looked. Together, we walked the rest of the way to the top and took our "after" photo at Bright Angel Trailhead. Then we headed to my uncle's home and were immediately given … you guessed it, ice cream cones!

Rim to Rim

The Finish

My sister, mom, Uncle and I near the South Rim

There is nothing like the feeling that the end of a long, challenging hike brings, and this trip really made me love backpacking even more. It was hard; it challenged my body, mind, and soul, but at the end of each day, I got to lie out under the stars, knowing that I had done a full day's work. There really isn't anything much better than that. Even with all the devices and technology, there is nothing better than walking, running, and using your own body to get to your destination.

No matter how many blisters I had at the end of the day, or how sore my muscles were, there was a sense of accomplishment and pride that made up for it.

I didn't break any records to make this hike successful. All I did was enjoy the natural world and leaving behind nothing but footprints. I'm a person that normally goes fast and hard on hikes, so I found it weird to take four days on a Rim to Rim hike, when other people do it in just eight hours. However, I found that just because we took twelve times as long, our hike was no less difficult or fun, and it didn't give us any less reason to be proud of ourselves. In fact, taking the extra days provided us more memories, more chance to experience nature, and more time to think about what we saw and experienced than I expected.

 While in the canyon, my Uncle and I thoroughly enjoyed our time together and didn't worry about things like time, pace, or the real world. For four days, I was in the Canyon, with the Canyon, and focusing only on the Canyon, and that was something valuable to me. I was in total harmony with the canyon, the sun, the wind, the flowing creeks, and the earth. As the old saying goes, you can take the girl out of the canyon, but you can't take the canyon out of the girl!

Final Observations

- When someone says, "you're almost there," it might not actually mean "you're almost there."
- Downhill makes your muscles hurt a lot worse than uphill
- No matter how many naps you take while backpacking, you can still sleep like a log through the entire night.

Made in the USA
Lexington, KY
11 October 2017